"This [...]
interna[...]
Professor of Philosophy, Boston College

"Pope Saint John Paul II was blessed by God with a truly extraordinary life; he was the example of someone who treasured the gift of his priesthood to the very end of his life. At his death he truly went 'to the house of the Father.' The meditations in *The Way of the Cross with St. John Paul II* will benefit those who knew the pope personally and met with him on the pastoral or administrative level, as well as those who only heard about him or have read about him. I find the meditations focused and prayerful, and I highly recommend them to parish communities, as well as to individuals, families, groups, and institutions like colleges, houses of religious formation, and seminaries." — *Father Ignatius Waindim, Rector, St. Thomas Aquinas Major Seminary, Bambui, Cameroon*

"This Way of the Cross sets before us the heroic virtues of Pope Saint John Paul II in following the Master. It provides inspiration to each one of us in our particular situation to live in the imitation of Christ." — *Father Jude Thaddeus Mbi, Foyer de Charité, Bonjongo, Cameroon*

The Way of the Cross

THE WAY OF
THE CROSS

with ST. JOHN PAUL II

FATHER HERBERT NIBA

With a foreword by George Weigel

Our Sunday Visitor
Huntington, Indiana

Nihil Obstat
Msgr. Michael Heintz, Ph.D.
Censor Librorum

Imprimatur
✠ Kevin C. Rhoades
Bishop of Fort Wayne-South Bend
October 3, 2019

The *Nihil Obstat* and *Imprimatur* are official declarations that a book is free from doctrinal or moral error. It is not implied that those who have granted the *Nihil Obstat* and *Imprimatur* agree with the contents, opinions, or statements expressed.

Every reasonable effort has been made to determine copyright holders of excerpted materials and to secure permissions as needed. If any copyrighted materials have been inadvertently used in this work without proper credit being given in one form or another, please notify Our Sunday Visitor in writing so that future printings of this work may be corrected accordingly.

Our Sunday Visitor Publishing Division, Our Sunday Visitor, Inc., 200 Noll Plaza, Huntington, IN 46750; www.osv.com; 1-800-348-2440

ISBN: 978-1-68192-595-0 (Inventory No. T2459)
1. RELIGION—Prayerbooks—Christian. 2. RELIGION—Holidays—Easter & Lent. 3. RELIGION—Christianity—Catholic.

LCCN: 2019949080

Cover and interior design: Lindsey Riesen
Cover art: Shutterstock, CNS photo by Michael Okoniewski

PRINTED IN THE UNITED STATES OF AMERICA

For the eternal repose of the victims of the Cameroon Anglophone Crisis (2016–), for a peaceful resolution of the root causes, and for the grace of healing on the afflicted communities.

Contents

SAINT JOHN PAUL II: THE STATIONS AND THE NEW EVANGELIZATION

The Basilica of St. Francis of Assisi in Kraków's Old Town is a short walk across the street from the residence of the city's archbishop. During the years he held that office, Archbishop (later Cardinal) Karol Wojtyła would walk across ul. Franciszkańska and enter the Gothic-style basilica beneath a great stained glass window crafted by Stanisław Wyspiański to depict God in the act of creation. Turning left into a side chapel, which features fourteen striking paintings of the *Via Crucis* (*Way of the Cross*) by Józef Mehoffer, the man who would become Pope John Paul II prayed the Stations of the Cross every Friday and every day during Lent.

That pattern continued in Rome, where John Paul II would also pray the Stations every Friday of the year and every day during Lent — when weather permitted, in a garden atop the Apostolic Palace. These habits tell us that the cross was at the center of Karol Wojtyła's Christocentric spirituality and that devotion to Christ, suffering and crucified, was formed very early in him.

As a son of Poland and its rich Catholic culture, Wojtyła, from the time he was a young boy, saw many sculptures of *Ecce Homo*, the scourged and thorn-crowned Christ dressed in a mock-royal robe, which is a prominent image in Polish artistic piety. Shortly after young Karol's mother died, his father took him to see the Passion play at Kalwaria Zebrzydowska, the outdoor Holy Land shrine near their home in Wadowice. There, the small boy saw a three-day-long depiction of the Lord's last week in which tens of thousands of Poles "participated," taking the place of the crowds who first acclaimed Jesus as their king and then called for his blood.

Later, as a young priest, Wojtyła would meditate on the great statue of Christ bearing the cross that stood before the Holy Cross Church in Warsaw. Like the rest of the city, the church had been destroyed by the Nazis in the aftermath of the 1944 Warsaw Uprising. But in 1946, when workers were digging through the rubble of what had once been the church, they found the statue almost completely intact and reinstalled it in front of the rebuilt church as a symbol of Poland risen from beneath the rubble of the Second World War and its horrors. Still later, when he visited the great Ark Church he had built in Nowa Huta, the "model communist city" outside Kraków that was deliberately planned to have no church, Cardinal Wojtyła saw yet another *Ecce Homo* image: this time, a metal sculpture cast from shrapnel and bullets taken from the bodies of Polish soldiers who had been wounded in the Battle of Monte Cassino in Italy in 1944.

This constant meditation on the Passion of the Lord taught John Paul II that the cross has power, and that the embrace of the cross empowers those who walk the *Via Crucis* to be apostles, witnesses to the truth, and agents of reconciliation in the world. To follow the Lord Jesus in abandoning oneself to the will of the Father and to accept in faith whatever pain and anxiety that abandonment might require is to enter into the mystery of redemptive suffering, which John Paul II explored in his 1984 apostolic letter *Salvifici Doloris*.

Suffering is a phenomenon unique to human beings. Animals feel pain; only human beings suffer. Suffering touches the soul and the heart and the mind, not only the body. Suffering thus has a spiritual dimension, which the world often misunderstands or ignores. But suffering embraced as a participation in the redemptive suffering of Christ, according to the pattern described by Saint Paul in Colossians 1:24, empowers us to share in the reconciliation that God effected through the cross and Resurrection and to offer to all we meet the possibility of sharing in that reconciliation.

The cross is thus an integral part of the New Evangelization. For as Saint Paul reminded the Corinthians, the true Gospel is the Gospel of "Jesus Christ and him crucified" (1 Cor 2:2). This has always been a "sign of contradiction," as Cardinal Wojtyła reminded the officials of the Roman Curia when, in 1976, he preached at their annual Lenten retreat at the invitation of Pope Paul VI. That is especially true today, when what Saint Teresa Benedicta of the Cross (Edith Stein) called the "science of the Cross" challenges, indeed contradicts, so much of what the world imagines to be true about the human condition and human happiness. But in calling the world to embrace the cross, the Church of the New Evangelization is calling humanity to recognize the truth about our lives: that we come to the fulfilment of our humanity by making ourselves into a gift for others, just as our own lives are a gift to us. The grace to be self-giving, which includes abandonment to the Father's providential will, is what enables us to embrace the life of the Beatitudes and to find the fulfilment of our happiness in doing so.

May these meditations, which enable us to walk the *Via Crucis* with Saint John Paul II, inspire the future priests of Africa to live the Great Commission of Matthew 28:19–20 and, in doing so, to inspire the entire world Church to a rediscovery of its evangelical identity and mission.

George Weigel
Distinguished Senior Fellow and William E. Simon
Chair in Catholic Studies
Ethics and Public Policy Center
Washington, DC
February 2018

Introduction

I grew up with a fascination for Pope John Paul II. My parents and siblings often recalled memories of his first visit to Cameroon in 1985, when he addressed pilgrims in several local dialects at the Bamenda Airport. When the pope visited Cameroon again in 1995, I could only watch him on television, but I was deeply moved to see him bend down and kiss the earth immediately after he stepped out of the plane. From then on, I knew there was something special about this pope. His death on April 2, 2005, coincided with the beginning of my seminary formation and spurred me to begin reading his books and other works about him. When his canonization fell on the same date as my first Thanksgiving Mass after my priestly ordination (Sunday, April 27, 2014), I knew that this developing love story was not just a set of coincidences but an invitation for me to follow the example of this beloved pope on my own journey toward the imitation of Christ. It was no surprise for me, therefore, that my first two priestly assignments were at the service of institutions dedicated to John Paul II: the first an institute of theology for the laity, and the second a major seminary. In the plan of God, there are no coincidences!

This Way of the Cross, therefore, is the fruit of several years of reflection on the life of John Paul II in the context of both personal spiritual reading and classroom teaching. I find it significant that my first contribution to further the legacy of this contemporary saint is a work of popular devotion. Praying the Way of the Cross is a practice dear to the Christians of the Bamenda Ecclesiastical Province where I grew up. It is a spiritual rendezvous every weekday of Lent, as well as during pilgrimages and other spiritual exercises. Many passages of the popular Pidgin English version are memorable and have become familiar words of spiritual admonition and personal motivation.

My aim in this little booklet is to give a new touch to this devotion and to inspire more persons to follow Christ using the life and witness of a man who himself prayed this prayer every Friday. When John Paul II was too weak to leave the Vatican to make the Stations of the Cross on his last Good Friday, he watched the annual procession in Rome from a television in his private chapel. A week later, on the day before his death, he signaled to those with him that he wanted once again to pray the Way of the Cross. As you read these reflections during private or public prayer, reflect on situations in your life where the Lord is challenging you to follow him, just as he challenged John Paul II. Above all, listen as John Paul II encourages you in the words of Saint Paul: "Be imitators of me, as I am of Christ" (1 Cor 11:1).

The communal celebration of this Way of the Cross requires about six liturgical ministers: three servers and three lectors. One server leads the way with a processional crucifix, flanked by two candle bearers. At each station, a leader announces the station and reads the opening Scripture and reflection, followed by a pair of lectors representing the witnesses at that station. The congregation joins in the concluding prayers. As circumstances permit, a hymn can be sung after each station. The choice to alternate postures (standing and kneeling) is left to the discretion of the community.

About the Witnesses

T his Way of the Cross contains fourteen witness testimonies, one for each station. The overall aim of including these testimonies is to create a true dialogue of prayer, where witnesses separated by time and place intersect in their portrait of the exemplary holiness of Saint John Paul II. These witnesses illuminate Karol Józef Wojtyła's life, from his boyhood in Wadowice in the 1920s, to his ministry as archbishop of Kraków, up to his funeral in Rome in 2005.

The witnesses chosen differ in time, status, and relationship to John Paul II. Some are still alive, while many are not. Most are real historical figures, and several are saints. One witness (at the tenth station) is a fictional character, based on real events from John Paul II's life. For clarity's sake, here is a breakdown of the witnesses and how their testimonies are included in each station:

- At the sixth, ninth, eleventh, and fourteenth stations, the words of the witnesses paraphrase direct words of the persons concerned.

- At the second, third, fifth, eighth, and twelfth stations, the testimonies come from life events recorded in biographical works on either John Paul II or the witness, and other stories recounted by the cited authors.

- At the first and thirteenth stations, the words are partly from the witnesses (as indicated) and partly attributions, yet all are historically rooted.

- At the tenth station, the witness is an artistic creation, but the words are from John Paul II's biography.

- At the third station, John Paul II speaks before the witness does; his words determined this.

Station	Witness	Relationship to Pope John Paul II
First	Cardinal Stefan Wyszyński (Pronounced *Vih-SHIN-skee*)	Cardinal primate of Poland from 1953 to 1981
Second	Monsignor Emery Kabongo	Assistant secretary to Pope John Paul II from 1982 to 1987; as of this writing, archbishop emeritus of Luebo, Democratic Republic of Congo
Third	Maria Kydryński (Pronounced *Kih-DRIN-skee*)	Childhood friend of Karol and neighbor to the Wojtyłas at Tyniecka Street, Kraków
Fourth	Jan Tyranowski (Pronounced *Teer-an-OV-skee*)	A tailor and lay mystic who inspired Karol Wojtyła's devotion to the Rosary and Carmelite spirituality

Station	Witness	Relationship to Pope John Paul II
Fifth	Quarry worker	Coworker at the Zakrzówek (pronounced *Zak-SHO-vek*) quarry, where Karol worked from 1940 to 1941 during the German occupation
Sixth	Michel Remery	1995 World Youth Day pilgrim from the Netherlands, as of this writing Father Michel Remery, priest of the Diocese of Rotterdam, the Netherlands
Seventh	Fallen-away priest	A priest reinstated to ministry by Pope John Paul II
Eighth	Pietro Molla	Husband of Saint Gianna Beretta Molla (1922–1962), the Italian doctor who sacrificed her life to save her unborn baby. She was canonized by Pope John Paul II in 2004.

Station	Witness	Relationship to Pope John Paul II
Ninth	Sister Maria Lúcia of Jesus	One of the three children (with Jacinta and Francisco) who received apparitions of Our Lady at Fátima in 1917, three years before Pope John Paul II was born. The vision narrated is the "third secret of Fátima."
Tenth	Patient in a hospital in Cameroon	Patient blessed by Pope John Paul II during his visit to Cameroon in 1985 (artistic creation)
Eleventh	Mother Teresa of Calcutta (Now Saint Teresa of Calcutta)	Born Albanian, founder of the Order of the Missionaries of Charity. She was beatified by Pope John Paul II on October 19, 2003.

Station	Witness	Relationship to Pope John Paul II
Twelfth	Sister Tobiana Sobótka (Pronounced *So-BOT-ka*)	Caretaker and nurse at the papal household
	Monsignor Stanisław Dziwisz (Pronounced *JEE-vish*)	Personal secretary of John Paul II when he was archbishop (1966–1978) and pope (1978–2005)
Thirteenth	Saint John Chrysostom (c. 349–407)	Early Christian preacher
Fourteenth	Monsignor Tadeuz Kondrusiewicz (pronounced *Ta-DE-oosh Kon-dru-SHYE-vich*)	Pilgrim at Pope John Paul II's funeral, ordained bishop by Pope John Paul II in Rome (1989). As of this writing, he is archbishop of Minsk-Mahilyow in Belarus.

THE WAY OF THE CROSS WITH ST. JOHN PAUL II

Prayer Before the Altar

Leader: In the name of the Father, and of the Son, and of the Holy Spirit.

Congregation: Amen.

Leader: We are gathered to celebrate the events of the final stage of the earthly journey of Our Lord. We will relive his Way of the Cross through the life of Saint John Paul II. Because John Paul II modeled his life intimately on the life of Christ, he was filled with courage and bore witness to the world of God's providence and mercy. As we begin our prayer, let us ask God for the grace to make this journey a true path of conversion and inspiration toward more authentic discipleship.

Do not be afraid to welcome and follow Christ!

Congregation: Open wide the doors to him and accept his saving power!

Leader: Let us pray.

Congregation: Lord Jesus, you called Saint John Paul II to be your servant and sent him all over the world to preach your Gospel. Be with us now as we imitate him who imitated you so well in your Way of the Cross. To you, Suffering Servant and Savior of the world, be praise and glory forever. Amen.

JESUS IS CONDEMNED TO DEATH

Leader: We adore you, O Christ, and we bless you.

Congregation: Because by your holy cross you have redeemed the world.

Leader: *Pilate then called together the chief priests and the rulers and the people. ... [He] addressed them ..., desiring to release Jesus; but they shouted out, "Crucify, crucify him!" ... [H]e said to them, "Why, what evil has he done? I have found in him no crime deserving death; I will therefore chastise him and release him." But they were urgent, demanding with loud cries that he should be crucified. ... So Pilate gave sentence that their demand should be granted. He released [Barabbas,] the man who had been thrown into prison for insurrection and murder, whom they asked for; but Jesus he delivered up to their will (Lk 23:13, 20–25).*

Pilate was the representative of Rome in Jerusalem. During the trial of Jesus, it was actually Pilate who was being judged. In Pilate, Our Lord scrutinized all judicial, political, and economic systems that remove

God from the center of life. Like Our Lord, who lived in a land occupied by rival nations, John Paul II also knew the torments of living in a land under foreign oppression. This reality shaped his whole journey of discipleship, from childhood to his ministry as pope.

Cardinal Stefan Wyszyński *(pronounced Vih-SHIN-skee)*: I still remember that conclave, the second in barely two months. In choosing Wojtyła, the cardinals, in a sense, chose Poland. After his election, the pope honored us by paying a visit to his homeland. If his election showed the judgment from the finger of God, then his visit to Poland pointed to where change would begin. From the very beginning, I knew what his cross would be — namely, to lead the Church into the third millennium.

Pope John Paul II: If God decided that a successor of Saint Peter should come from Poland, that meant that there was something about the experience of Poland that could be relevant to the Church. I was spared much of the horrible drama of the Second World War. I could have been arrested any day and taken away to a concentration camp. Sometimes I would ask myself: So many people my own age are losing their lives; *why not me*? Today I know that it was not mere chance.

Leader: Before I formed you in the womb I knew you.

Congregation: And before you were born I consecrated you (Jer 1:5).

Leader: Let us pray.

Congregation: Lord Jesus, you have taught us that God has no favorites and that anybody of any nationality who fears him and does what is right is acceptable to him. Teach us to know that we have each been created for a particular mission, and give us the grace to follow you wherever your call leads us. You who live and reign forever and ever. Amen.

***

JESUS TAKES UP HIS CROSS

Leader: We adore you, O Christ, and we bless you.

Congregation: Because by your holy cross you have redeemed the world.

Leader: *So they took Jesus, and he went out, bearing his own cross, to the place called the place of a skull, which is called in Hebrew Gol'gotha (Jn 19:17).*

Jesus said, "If any man would come after me, let him deny himself and take up his cross daily and follow me" (Lk 9:23). John Paul II responded to this invitation many times. Each response seemed to take him away from something he deeply loved, such as his early involvement in theater and poetry, and his pastoral engagement with youth. But since the love of Christ was the dominant force of his life, he was able to bear each new task, even that task that transcends mere human ability — that of being a shepherd of Christ's flock, his universal Church.

Monsignor Emery Kabongo: He was a man of prayer. A cardinal called one night at three in the morning to alert the pope of an international emergency. I searched for the pope in the bedroom, chapel, kitchen, and private library, but could not find him. Fear overtook me. Then I retraced my steps and finally found him in the chapel, lying prostrate on the floor, praying. His stamina to carry his cross came from his intimate union with God.

Pope John Paul II: The one about to receive holy orders prostrates himself completely and rests his forehead on the church floor. In this way, he indicates his complete willingness to undertake the ministry being entrusted to him. This rite has deeply marked my priestly life. Lying on the floor in the form of a cross is a way of accepting in one's own life the cross of Christ and becoming a "floor" for our brothers and sisters. When a man says *yes* to God, that *yes* is forever!

Leader: You did not choose me, but I chose you.

Congregation: And appointed you that you should go and bear fruit and that your fruit should abide (Jn 15:16).

Leader: Let us pray.

Congregation: Lord Jesus, you carried your own cross, and you ask us to follow you on this path. Help us to see in the cross not only the symbol of suffering but also the power of God to save. May we glory in your cross, you who are our life, our hope, and our salvation. Amen.

Third Station

JESUS FALLS THE FIRST TIME

Leader: We adore you, O Christ, and we bless you.

Congregation: Because by your holy cross you have redeemed the world.

Leader: *I am the man who has seen affliction
   under the rod of his wrath; …
he has blocked my ways with hewn stones (Lam 3:1, 9).*

*Friend and neighbor you have taken away,
My one companion is darkness (Ps 88:18, Grail).*

A fall is a setback on one's journey, a time of trial, a test of faith. Jesus promised us not a smooth discipleship, but one filled with much suffering. In Jesus' fall beneath the weight of the cross, the meaning of his whole life is seen: He emptied himself and became obedient unto death for our sake. John Paul II also had several setbacks on his Way of the Cross. His early life was marked by repeated personal tragedy. His faith was tested. Like Christ, he abandoned himself to the will of the Father.

Pope John Paul II: I had not made my first Communion when I lost my mother: I was barely nine years old. After her death and, later, the death of my older brother, I was left alone with my father, a deeply religious man. He was a retired soldier, and after my mother's death his life became one of constant prayer. We never spoke of a vocation to the priesthood, but his example was in a way my first seminary, a kind of domestic seminary. One day, returning from the quarry, I went to give him his medicine, but found him dead. At twenty, I had already lost all the people I had loved.

Maria Kydryński *(pronounced Kih-DRIN-skee)*: I was there with Karol when he discovered his father was dead, and I helped to get a priest to anoint him. Karol spent an entire night on his knees beside his father's body, praying and weeping like I had never seen him do before. Because he was the last surviving member of his immediate family, the death of "Captain," as we nicknamed his father, was a blow that struck Karol badly. But the experience renewed his confidence in God. Emerging from it in hope, he stood up tall and embraced the new family God had for him.

Leader: Fear not, for I am with you (Is 41:10).

Congregation: Rise, let us be going (Mk 14:42).

Leader: Let us pray.

Congregation: Lord Jesus, you promise us that whoever abandons everything to follow you will receive blessings a hundredfold, but not without persecutions. Help us to rise each time we fall and take the cross rather than shun it. May we never complain or become discouraged by life's trials. Make us follow your path of love and, in submitting to its demands, find joy. Amen.

Fourth Station

JESUS MEETS HIS SORROWFUL MOTHER

Leader: We adore you, O Christ, and we bless you.

Congregation: Because by your holy cross you have redeemed the world.

Leader: *[A]nd Simeon blessed them and said to Mary his mother, "Behold, this child is set for the fall and rising of many in Israel, and for a sign that is spoken against (and a sword will pierce through your own soul also), that thoughts out of many hearts may be revealed" (Lk 2:34–35).*

As Mary saw Our Lord in agony on his Way of the Cross, she knew in her heart that his hour had come. No one understands more than Mary God's love for the struggling sinner. Mary also stands with us and with all the afflicted, for she is the Mother of Sorrows. At the same time, she is the cause of our joy, for she renewed her *yes* to God, even while seeing her Son bathed in sweat and blood. That is why John Paul II entrusted his whole life to her.

Jan Tyranowski *(pronounced Teer-an-OV-skee)*: During the war, I was asked to coordinate our parish youth ministry after the deportation of the clergy. This saw the birth of the Living Rosary, whose members consecrated themselves to Our Lady and embarked upon a life of intense prayer and service to others. Karol was one of its first leaders. He joined us on pilgrimages to the major shrines, where, as he put it, he would go to hear the Mother's "heartbeat." It was this intimacy with Mary that made him grasp deeply the mysteries of Christ.

Pope John Paul II: At first, it had seemed to me that I should distance myself a bit from the Marian devotion of my childhood in order to focus more on Christ. But thanks to Saint Louis-Marie de Montfort, I came to understand that true devotion to the Mother of God is actually Christ-centered. Mary leads us to Christ, but at the same time, Christ leads us to his Mother, who in a certain sense was crucified spiritually with her crucified Son.

Leader: *Totus tuus*: I am all yours, Mary.

Congregation: And all that is mine is yours.

Leader: Let us pray.

Congregation: Mary, my Mother, pray for me and for all your children who are so deeply in need of the mercy of your Son, which was poured out from the cross for the redemption of the world. Teach, lead, and guide me, so that I may incline my heart to live in union with Christ always. Amen.

Fifth Station

SIMON OF CYRENE HELPS JESUS CARRY THE CROSS

Leader: We adore you, O Christ, and we bless you.

Congregation: Because by your holy cross you have redeemed the world.

Leader: *And as [the soldiers] led him away, they seized one Simon of Cyre'ne, who was coming in from the country, and laid on him the cross, to carry it behind Jesus (Lk 23:26).*

The soldiers forced Simon of Cyrene to help Jesus carry the cross, although Simon did not intend it. In this brief encounter, the mystery of Jesus, silent and suffering, touched Simon's heart. He participated in the work of God for our salvation. Like Simon, John Paul II knew that whenever we show kindness to the suffering, the persecuted, and the defenseless, we help to carry the same cross of Jesus. People need solidarity. When we participate in the lives of others, we become authentically human and Christian.

Quarry worker: At the quarry, all of us could figure out that Karol was different. But he became one of us and came to know our living situations, our families, our interests, our human work, and our dignity. Later, as a priest and bishop, he baptized our children, blessed their marriages, and officiated at many funerals. He also showed solidarity with our trade unions and at times suffered for doing so. He was like Simon of Cyrene to us, a true companion on our journey.

Pope John Paul II: My experience at the stone quarry was a kind of a spiritual seminary. I interacted daily with people who did heavy work and appreciated their quiet religiosity and great wisdom about life. Here I began to think more deeply about the meaning of work itself, seeing it not so much as a curse of original sin but rather as a "participation in God's creativity." Our Lord, who did not disdain being called the "son of a carpenter," proclaimed the Gospel not only by words but by deeds.

Leader: Bear one another's burdens.

Congregation: And so fulfill the law of Christ (Gal 6:2).

Leader: Let us pray.

Congregation: Lord Jesus, grant us the strength and courage to share your cross and your sufferings in our daily life and work with others. Give us a spirit of service and sacrifice, that we may not seek power and glory but strive to be an instrument of solidarity for those crushed by the violence and injustice of the powerful of this world. Amen.

VERONICA WIPES THE FACE OF JESUS

Leader: We adore you, O Christ, and we bless you.

Congregation: Because by your holy cross you have redeemed the world.

Leader: *You have said, "Seek my face."*
   My heart says to you,
"Your face, LORD, do I seek."
   Hide not your face from me (Ps 27:8–9).

For the one who truly loves God, no sacrifice can be too great. Veronica is a true icon of those who are able to receive, return, and radiate the love of God. Disregarding the cruelty of Our Lord's tormentors and the crowd of onlookers, she made her way to Jesus and wiped his face with a towel. As John Paul II said, those who seek after Christ, who open wide their doors to him, lose nothing; in fact, they gain everything! Veronica returned with the image of Christ. In the same way, those who encountered the pope, both young and old, never returned the same: He showed them the face of Christ.

Michel Remery: I was asked to deliver a message in the presence of the pope in the name of the youth of the world. There were so many people that moving a few inches in any direction was extremely difficult. Yet we did. Before leaving my country, I thought the pope was an old man who just talked of what you weren't supposed to do. But the more I listened to him, the more I realized that he loved us deeply and really wanted us to know and love Christ all the more. He even told us not to be afraid to become saints. Yes, to be saints of the new millennium!

Pope John Paul II: What explains the millions of youth that gathered for the World Youth Days? There can be only one answer: They are searching for God and for the meaning of life. The more the world deprives them of what is true, good, and beautiful, the more earnestly they yearn for it. This explains why they flock to the World Youth Days. They are looking for Jesus Christ! Only Christ knows "that which is in every man;" only he can give true answers to man's deepest questions. The Church needs the enthusiasm of the young. She needs the courage to be like Veronica.

Leader: Behold, I stand at the door and knock.

Congregation: If any one hears my voice and opens the door, I will come in to him and eat with him, and he with me (Rv 3:20).

Leader: Let us pray.

Congregation: Lord Jesus, you have taught us that

whoever asks, receives; whoever searches, finds; and whoever knocks will have the door opened. May I, like Veronica, be able to seek you more fervently, love you more dearly, and follow you more closely. Grant that I may be able to recognize your face even in the afflicted and the oppressed and serve you in them. Amen.

Seventh Station

JESUS FALLS A SECOND TIME

Leader: We adore you, O Christ, and we bless you.

Congregation: Because by your holy cross you have redeemed the world.

Leader: *Surely he has borne our griefs*
and carried our sorrows; …
[H]e was wounded for our transgressions,
he was bruised for our iniquities;
upon him was the chastisement that made us whole,
and with his stripes we are healed (Is 53:4–6).

Jesus fell in the person of his disciples each time they failed to keep their promises or tried to exclude others from his mission. Their lack of faith sometimes broke Our Lord's heart. As we try to imitate Christ, we are confronted with our weaknesses and those of others, which add more thorns to Our Lord's crown. John Paul II encountered his share of such thorns; on several occasions, he asked and offered pardon on behalf of the Church. In this way, he invited each of us to renew daily our resolve to follow Christ.

Fallen-away priest: After undergoing a crisis, I crashed and burned in my vocation and left the priesthood. Things turned worse, and I became a beggar in front of a basilica in Rome. Then someone arranged a meeting with the pope for me. To my shock, the pope (instead of scolding me) clasped my hands and insisted that I hear his confession. Despite my initial objection, I absolved him and knelt at his feet, and he did the same for me. He restored my faculties and assigned me to minister to other beggars in the city. The healing power of forgiveness became my greatest miracle. The grace of God has never again been fruitless in me.

Pope John Paul II: Although she is holy because of her incorporation into Christ, the Church does not tire of doing penance. Even an undefiled mother sheds tears at the sins of her children. The Church must humbly ask forgiveness on behalf of so many of her children who have sullied her face. At the same time, she must rely on the power of the Lord, who fills her with the gift of holiness, leads her forward, and conforms her to his Passion and resurrection.

Leader: No human sin can erase the mercy of God.

Congregation: For the lowliest man may be pardoned in mercy (Ws 6:6).

Leader: Let us pray.

Congregation: Lord Jesus, by falling a second time and rising again on your Way of the Cross, you teach me that you are a God of second chances. By the merits of your Passion, do not allow me to rely on my tears or to be driven by pride. Grant me, rather, the courage to rise and take the path of conversion. You who live and reign forever and ever. Amen.

Eighth Station

JESUS MEETS THE WOMEN OF JERUSALEM

Leader: We adore you, O Christ, and we bless you.

Congregation: Because by your holy cross you have redeemed the world.

Leader: *And there followed him a great multitude of the people, and of women who bewailed and lamented him. But Jesus turning to them said, "Daughters of Jerusalem, do not weep for me, but weep for yourselves and for your children" (Lk 23:27–28).*

The tears of the women of Jerusalem accompany the sorrowful journey of Our Lord. These tears are but a small drop in the river of tears shed by women of every generation: tears of the mothers of broken homes, tears of the mothers of criminals, tears of the mothers of victims of crimes, tears of displaced persons. Our Lord's reply to the women shows that tears are never enough; tears must overflow into a love that nurtures, a firmness that corrects, a dialogue that heals, and a presence that speaks. Tears must prevent other tears. Like Our Lord, John Paul II recognized not only the dignity of women as disciples but also the witness of those who went beyond mere compassion to enact heroic discipleship.

Pietro Molla: My wife, Gianna, was diagnosed with uterine cancer during her fourth pregnancy. As a mother, she knew that she was *necessary* to me and her three children but *indispensable* to the baby she carried in her womb. She prayed and prayed, and asked for the grace to be ready to do the will of God. Before her surgery, she told the doctors, "Save the child, not me." After a painful night of labor, the birth took place on Holy Saturday morning. She gazed at our newborn girl, held her close, and silently caressed her with indescribable tenderness. Gianna died a week after. The grain of wheat had borne fruit but not without cost. Like Christ, she was faithful in her love until death (cf. Rv 2:10).

Pope John Paul II: Love is the most beautiful sentiment the Lord has put into the souls of men and women. Only those who have the courage to give of themselves totally to God and to others are able to fulfill themselves.

Leader: Can a woman forget her sucking child, that she should have no compassion on the son of her womb?

Congregation: Even these may forget, yet I will not forget you (Is 49:15).

Leader: Let us pray.

Congregation: Lord Jesus, through the women of Jerusalem, you teach us the seriousness of our responsibility as disciples. Give us strength, even in this valley of tears, to bear courageous witness to you beyond mere compassionate words. Make every Christian family a true school of mercy, discipleship, and faithful love. Amen.

JESUS FALLS THE THIRD TIME

Leader: We adore you, O Christ, and we bless you.

Congregation: Because by your holy cross you have redeemed the world.

Leader: *Are you not from everlasting,*
*   O LORD my God, my Holy One? ...*
[W]hy do you look on faithless men,
*   and are silent when the wicked swallows up*
*   the man more righteous than he? ...*
And the LORD answered me:
"Write the vision;
*   make it plain upon tablets. ...*
For still the vision awaits its time; ...
If it seem slow, wait for it;
it will surely come, it will not delay.
Behold, he whose soul is not upright in him shall fail,
*   but the righteous shall live by his faith (Hb 1:12–13;*
*   2:2–4).*

Our Lord Jesus said, "'A servant is not greater than his master.' If they persecuted me, they will persecute you"

(Jn 15:20). On the evening of May 13, 1981, Pope John Paul II was greeting and blessing some pilgrims and tourists after the weekly papal audience. A gunman fired two bullets at the pope, one hitting him directly in the abdomen and the other fracturing his index finger. The pope fell and was rushed to the hospital, but he recovered miraculously. Like his Master, John Paul II had become both priest and victim.

Sister Maria Lúcia of Jesus: My cousins, Jacinta and Francisco, and I were shepherd children at Fátima. One day, Our Lady showed us a vision. A bishop, dressed in white, was passing through a city half in ruins to climb a steep mountain. While kneeling at prayer at the foot of a big cross, he was shot by bullets fired by soldiers. We did not know which pope the vision referred to, and that made us suffer. Beneath the arms of the cross, two angels gathered up the blood of the martyrs in a vessel and with it sprinkled the souls that were making their way to God.

Pope John Paul II: When I was wounded by gunshots fired in St. Peter's Square, at first I did not pay attention to the fact that the attempt on my life occurred on the exact anniversary of Our Lady's appearance to the three children at Fátima. But all along, I had a vivid presentiment that I would be saved. I asked the world to pray for my would-be assassin, whom I had sincerely forgiven. One hand fired, but another hand, Mary's hand, guided the bullet.

Leader: Blessed are those who are persecuted for righteousness' sake.

Congregation: For theirs is the kingdom of heaven (Mt 5:10).

Leader: Let us pray.

Congregation: Lord, as you fell on your Way of the Cross, your disciples also fall. In our days, as in times past, attacks against your Church and against Christians are on the rise. Console us for the sorrow they bring and awaken in all believers your call to conversion. May the blood of martyrs sow a living seed of peace among nations and freedom of religion. Amen.

JESUS IS STRIPPED OF HIS GARMENTS

Leader: We adore you, O Christ, and we bless you.

Congregation: Because by your holy cross you have redeemed the world.

Leader: *And when [the soldiers] had mocked him, they stripped him of the purple cloak, and put his own clothes on him. And they led him out to crucify him (Mk 15:20).*

Our Lord, who was the "fairest of the sons of men" (Ps 45:2), is now without beauty. The holy face that dazzled his apostles at the Transfiguration is now bruised, derided, cursed, and defiled. John Paul II also knew this transformation. As a young man and even in his early days as pope, he was of great physical stamina and charm. But his failing health and suffering aged him quickly. His figure was bent, and he needed support from his pastoral staff. Later, several surgeries and Parkinson's disease rendered both his speech and movement difficult. Like Our Lord, he had become a man of sorrows, acquainted with grief.

Patient in a hospital in Cameroon: The pope often visited the sick and asked for their prayers. He believed that the weak are a great source of strength for the Church. For him, Christians should not only *do good to those who suffer* but also *do good by their suffering.* I was happy to have been blessed by him in the hospital. When he was with the sick and old, he was never in a hurry.

Pope John Paul II: When confronted with suffering, most of us ask: "Why? Why me? Why now?" Christ does not explain in the abstract the reasons for suffering. Before all else, he says: "Follow me. Come. Take part through your suffering in this work of saving the world." Gradually, as the individual takes up his cross, spiritually uniting himself to the cross of Christ, the salvific meaning of suffering is revealed before him.

Leader: Now I rejoice in my sufferings for your sake.

Congregation: And in my flesh, I complete what is lacking in Christ's afflictions for the sake of his body, that is, the Church (Col 1:24).

Leader: Let us pray.

Congregation: Lord Jesus, you underwent humiliation to give us glory. Help us to see in your cross the victory of your love, so that we may neither shun nor waste pain. May we recognize that every infirmity carries a message and that your Passion has given human suffering new meaning and dignity. Amen.

Eleventh Station

JESUS IS NAILED TO THE CROSS

Leader: We adore you, O Christ, and we bless you.

Congregation: Because by your holy cross you have redeemed the world.

Leader: *And they crucified him, and divided his garments among them, casting lots for them, to decide what each should take. ... And with him they crucified two robbers, one on his right and one on his left. And those who passed by derided him, shaking their heads, and saying: "Aha! You who would destroy the temple and build it in three days, save yourself, and come down from the cross!" (Mk 15:24, 27–30).*

The hands and feet of Jesus are nailed to the cross, the very hands that blessed everyone, and the feet that walked everywhere bringing life and love. Despite the voices tempting him from below to come down from the cross, he does not shun death, but willingly embraces it. Like Christ, John Paul II's profound union with God was revealed even in the last moments of his life. He remained strong in spirit and loved until the end (cf. Jn 13:1). When asked by some to resign, he answered back: "Jesus did not descend from the cross, why should I? I have to make it to the end."

Mother Teresa of Calcutta: The Lord wanted John Paul II beside him on the cross to remind the world that only in the cross is there resurrection and life. With the ailing pope in the hospital, the Lord showed us how he, too, crucified in the flesh, unites himself with all those in the world who bear the marks of the Passion of Jesus Christ. The work of redemption continues in time and in the life of every man and woman only through the embrace of the cross. After the cross comes the radiant dawn of the Resurrection.

Pope John Paul II: At my inauguration as pope, I made a fervent and trusting prayer: "O Christ, make me become and remain the servant of your unique power, the servant of your sweet power, the servant of your power that knows no eventide." Now, I ask him to call me back when he himself chooses. In life and death, we belong to the Lord. We are the Lord's (cf. Rom 14:8).

Leader: I have been crucified with Christ.

Congregation: It is no longer I who live, but Christ who lives in me (Gal 2:20).

Leader: Let us pray.

Congregation: Lord Jesus, you said, "When I am lifted up from the earth, [I] will draw all men to myself" (Jn 12:32). Do not let our faith be crushed in moments of pain and trial. Grant that we may lovingly accept your will and place ourselves each day in your merciful hands. Amen.

Twelfth Station

JESUS DIES ON THE CROSS

Leader: We adore you, O Christ, and we bless you.

Congregation: Because by your holy cross you have redeemed the world.

Leader: *It was now about the sixth hour, and there was darkness over the whole land until the ninth hour, while the sun's light failed; and the curtain of the temple was torn in two. Then Jesus, crying with a loud voice, said, "Father, into your hands I commit my spirit!" And having said this he breathed his last (Lk 23:44–46).*

The saints are raised to the altar not because they have conquered the world but because they have allowed Christ to conquer them. In his life, John Paul II taught the world how to live for Christ. In his death, he taught the world how to die in Christ.

Sister Tobiana Sobótka *(pronounced So-BOT-ka)***:** As he lay dying on his bed, the pope asked that the Gospel of John be read aloud to him. Then he beckoned to me and spoke his last words, saying in Polish, "Let me go to the house of the Father." By seven o'clock in the evening, he slipped into a coma. Shortly afterwards, Monsignor Dziwisz began celebrating Holy Mass — the vigil of the Feast of the Divine Mercy. A few drops of the Precious Blood were given to the holy father as Viaticum. After this, his heart stopped beating. He died just as he was born eighty-four years earlier — with the sounds of people singing prayers outside his window.

Pope John Paul II: Jesus' cry on the cross is not the cry of anguish of a man without hope but the prayer of the Son who offers his life to the Father in love, for the salvation of all. He is not abandoned by the Father; rather, he "abandons" himself to the Father with a last cry: "Father, into your hands I commit my spirit." These words close the mystery of the Passion and open up the mystery of liberation through death. May these words be our last words too, to open eternity to us.

Leader: Father, into your hands I commit my spirit (Lk 23:46).

Congregation: Do with me whatever you will.

Leader: Let us pray.

Congregation: Heavenly Father, your Son taught us how to live and how to die. In life as in death, he abandoned himself to your will. Make us believe that death no longer has the final word but is the passage to the fullness of life with you. Grant this through the same Christ Our Lord. Amen.

JESUS IS TAKEN DOWN FROM THE CROSS

Leader: We adore you, O Christ, and we bless you.

Congregation: Because by your holy cross you have redeemed the world.

Leader: *[S]tanding by the cross of Jesus were his mother, and his mother's sister, Mary the wife of Clopas, and Mary Mag'dalene. ... [T]he soldiers came and broke the legs of the first, and of the other who had been crucified with him; but when they came to Jesus and saw that he was already dead, they did not break his legs. But one of the soldiers pierced his side with a spear, and at once there came out blood and water. ... After this Joseph of Arimathe'a ... asked Pilate that he might take away the body of Jesus, and Pilate gave him leave (Jn 19:25, 32–34, 38).*

Our Lady accompanied her Son from his birth to his death. She saw the last gift Christ gave to the world — the water and blood from his side. John Paul II knew that the key to living a Christlike life is to enroll in the school of Mary, who contemplated her Son from his birth to his death.

Saint John Chrysostom: When two persons who love each other deeply are about to be separated for a while, they give each other a gesture or picture to prolong their presence to each other, despite the physical absence. At his death, Our Lord also gave us a supreme gift. From his pierced side, there flowed water and blood, symbols for baptism and the Eucharist. On the cross of Calvary, he sealed the gift of himself already given at the Last Supper. The Church draws its strength from the Eucharist. Jesus is indeed with us until the end of time!

Pope John Paul II: What must Mary have felt when she heard from the apostles the words spoken by Christ at the Last Supper: "This is my body which is given for you" (Lk 22:19)? The body broken at that table was the same body she had conceived in her womb, for she was the first tabernacle in history! At the foot of the cross, she welcomed again that body whose heart once beat in unison with hers.

Leader: Unless a grain of wheat falls into the earth and dies, it remains alone.

Congregation: But if it dies, it bears much fruit (Jn 12:24).

Leader: Let us pray.

Congregation: Lord Jesus, in the Eucharist you left us a memorial of your Passion. Help us to reverence the mystery of your Body and Blood, that we may always experience in our lives the fruit of your redemption. Who live and reign forever and ever. Amen.

JESUS IS LAID IN THE TOMB

Leader: We adore you, O Christ, and we bless you.

Congregation: Because by your holy cross you have redeemed the world.

Leader: *[Joseph of Arimathea] wrapped [Jesus] in the linen shroud, and laid him in a tomb which had been hewn out of the rock; and he rolled a stone against the door of the tomb (Mk 15:46).*

By lying in the grave, the Son of Man blessed the grave as a resting place to await the resurrection from the dead. After the funeral of John Paul II, a silent and devout pilgrimage continued to his tomb. Many pilgrims left behind little notes, like flower petals, in which they opened their hearts, offering him their sorrows and asking for his intercession. For many, he was a "saint" already. They believed that, like Christ, he had passed "from life into life."

Monsignor Tadeuz Kondrusiewcz *(pronounced Ta-DE-oosh Kon-dru-SHYE-vich)***:** I was present at St. Peter's Basilica when the dead body of the pope was

presented for viewing. It was so moving to see count-
less mourners line up for over twenty hours just to
walk past the open coffin, with many going for confession as they waited. It was like a worldwide retreat,
a posthumous audience with the pope. He longed to
see people open their hearts to Christ, and his wish
was truly accomplished. Having died with Christ, he
now awaited the Resurrection.

Pope John Paul II: After my priestly ordination on the
Feast of All Saints, 1946, I celebrated my Thanksgiving
Mass on All Souls' Day in the Crypt of Saint Leonard
in Wawel Cathedral at Kraków. This was to express
my spiritual bonds with the generations of Christians
buried there, and also a liturgical expression of my
belief in the communion of saints. All the baptized
whose mortal remains rest beneath the ground lie
there in "expectation of the resurrection of the body
and life everlasting." This is our faith; this is the faith
of the Church!

Leader: Indeed, for your faithful, Lord, life is changed,
not ended.

Congregation: When this earthly dwelling turns to
dust, an eternal dwelling is made for them in heaven.

Leader: Let us pray.

Congregation: Lord Jesus, your story does not end in
the tomb, for we believe you rose again on the third
day. On Easter Sunday, your empty tomb will be the
first sign of the victory of good over evil and of life
over death. May we who have accompanied you in

your Passion through the footsteps of your servant John Paul II find true joy in serving you on this earth and, at the last, see you face-to-face with your saints in glory. Amen.

PRAYER BEFORE THE ALTAR

Leader: Let us pray.

Congregation: O Blessed Trinity, we thank you for having graced the Church with Saint John Paul II and for allowing the tenderness of your fatherly care, the glory of the cross of Christ, and the splendor of the Spirit of love to shine through him. Trusting fully in your infinite mercy and in the maternal intercession of Mary, he has given us a living image of Jesus the Good Shepherd. He has shown us that holiness is the necessary measure of ordinary Christian life and is the way of achieving eternal communion with you. Grant us, by his intercession and according to your will, the graces we implore, through Christ Our Lord. Amen.

Leader: In the name of the Father, and of the Son, and of the Holy Spirit.

Congregation: Amen.

Acknowledgments

I thank God Almighty for the life and witness of Saint John Paul II and for inspiring me to write this work. I render thanks to my bishop, Monsignor Immanuel Bushu, who, after ordaining me, appointed me to two successive institutions dedicated to this great saint. I thank my fellow lecturers and students at St. John Paul II Institute of Theology, Buea, Cameroon, and St. John Paul II Major Seminary, Bachuo Ntai, Mamfe, Cameroon, for the spiritual environment they afforded me to complete this reflection.

The pattern of this Way of the Cross is inspired by Eugene A. LaVerdiere, SSS, who in four volumes wrote Jesus' Way of the Cross as portrayed by the evangelists Matthew, Luke, and John and by Saint Paul. Each volume featured a meditation on the Passion story from the perspective of those who crossed the path of Jesus and followed him to his death and resurrection. I have made a similar attempt here by interpreting Jesus' Way of the Cross using real situations from the life of Saint John Paul II supported by testimonies of persons who met him or whom he had the grace of raising to the altar as saints. I am indebted to Father LaVerdiere (1936–2008) for this approach.

The first draft of this work underwent the scrutiny of several persons, among whom I mention Fathers H. Peeters, M. Suh Niba, I. Waindim, C. Pishangu,

M. Ngantchop, T. Chi, J. Agbortoko, J. Berinyuy, and E. Gami. I take full responsibility for any errors still found in the final print. The moral support of Fathers K. Sakwe, J. Ngome, E. Nsaikila, M. Bamenjo, B. Ehinack, M. Agbaw-Ebai, as well as Sister B. Efembele, A. Ndumbe, L. Foleng, and M. Atong sustained me during the writing. I remain ever grateful to George Weigel, author of the authoritative biography of John Paul II, *A Witness to Hope*, who graced this work with a foreword.

Last but not least, I thank my family, in whose company I first prayed the Way of the Cross. I bless them for teaching me how to pray and for accompanying me through every step of my priestly journey. To all whose names I cannot mention and whose love and support I have enjoyed I ask the Lord to grant his choicest blessings!

This work is written at a time when my country is experiencing a deep sociopolitical crisis that has brought much pain, displacement of families, and loss of lives. It is my prayer that Saint John Paul II, who himself lived through two world wars and so became a great apostle of peace, freedom, human rights, and the dignity of the human person, may intercede to God for a lasting solution to the crisis in Cameroon, just as he was instrumental in bringing about change and healing in his homeland, Poland.

Father Herbert Niba Cheo
Mamfe, Cameroon
Feast of the Presentation of Our Lord
February 2, 2019

References

FIRST STATION

"In choosing Wojtyła … "	Michael O'Carroll, *Poland and John Paul II* (Dublin, Ireland: Veritas Publications, 1979), vii.
" … to lead the Church into … "	John Paul II, *Spiritual Testament,* Vatican website, March 17, 2000, w2.vatican.va, §1; Stanisław Dziwisz, *A Life with Karol: My Forty-Year Friendship with the Man Who Became Pope*, trans. Adrian Walker (New York: Doubleday, 2007), 61.
"If God decided that … "	George Weigel, *Witness to Hope: The Biography of Pope John Paul II, 1920–2005* (New York: Harper, 2005), 11.
" … it was not mere chance."	John Paul II, *Gift and Mystery: On the Fiftieth Anniversary of My Priestly Ordination* (New York: Doubleday, 1996), 36.

SECOND STATION

" … lying prostrate on the floor, praying … "	Timothy Dolan, *Priests for the Third Millenium* (Huntington, IN: Our Sunday Visitor, 2000), 61.
" … becoming a 'floor' for our brothers and sisters."	John Paul II, *Gift and Mystery*, 44, 46.
" … that *yes* is forever!"	John Paul II, "Homily for Priestly Ordination," Rome 1995.

THIRD STATION

"My one companion is darkness."	*The Divine Office: The Liturgy of the Hours according to the Roman Rite* (Dublin: Collins, 1974). *The Revised Grail Psalms,* (Conception Abbey, 2010).
" … a kind of domestic seminary."	John Paul II, *Gift and Mystery*, 36–37.
" … already lost all the people I had loved."	Gian Franco Svidercoschi, *Stories of Karol: The Unknown Life of John Paul II*, trans. Peter Heinegg (Liguori, MO: Liguori/Triumph, 2003), 38.

" … like I had never seen him do before."	Svidercoschi, *Stories of Karol*, 38.

FOURTH STATION

" … he would go to hear the Mother's 'heartbeat.'"	Dziwisz, *A Life with Karol*, 12.
" … true devotion to the Mother of God is actually Christ-centered."	John Paul II, *Crossing the Threshold of Hope* (New York: Alfred A. Knopf, 1994), 213.
" … Christ leads us to his Mother … "	John Paul II, *Gift and Mystery*, 28.
" … was crucified spiritually with her crucified Son."	Jason Evert, *Saint John Paul the Great: His Five Loves* (Lakewood, CO: Totus Tuus Press, 2014), 166.
"Totus tuus … "	John Paul II, *Gift and Mystery*, 30. Quoted in Latin as *"Totus Tuus ego sum et omnia mea Tua sunt."* Translation offered in Evert, *Saint John Paul the Great*, 166 ("I am all yours, and all that is mine is yours.").

FIFTH STATION

" … our human work, and our dignity."	John Paul II, *Gift and Mystery*, 22.
" … 'participation in God's creativity.'"	John Paul II, *Laborem Exercens*, encyclical letter, Vatican website, September 14, 1981, w2.vatican.va, §26.

SIXTH STATION

" … know and love Christ all the more."	Pawel Zuchniewicz, *Miracles of John Paul II*, trans. Paul Bulas et al. (Ontario, Canada: Catholic Youth Studio-KSM, 2006), 144–148.
" … to be saints of the new millennium!"	John Paul II, *Message of the Holy Father to the Youth of the World on the Occasion of the 15ᵗʰ World Youth Day*, message, Vatican website, June 29, 1999, w2.vatican.va.

" … and for the meaning of life."	John Paul II, *Crossing the Threshold of Hope*, 121. See also *Credo: John Paul II*, directed by Alberto Michelini (Italy: Sugar Productions, 2006), DVD. The Pope's words (Closing of the Youth Jubilee): "Who have you come to look for? There can be but one answer. You have come to search for Christ!" (23:23–23:48).
"They are looking for Jesus Christ!"	John Paul II, *Closing of World Youth Day*, homily, Vatican website, August 20, 2000, w2.vatican.va. See also *Credo: John Paul II*, DVD.
" … true answers to man's deepest questions."	John Paul II, *Crossing the Threshold of Hope*, 124–25.

Seventh Station

"After undergoing a crisis … "	Evert, *Saint John Paul the Great*, 190. See also Scott Hahn, *Lord, Have Mercy: The Healing Power of Confession* (New York: Doubleday, 2003).

"Even an undefiled mother sheds tears at the sins of her children."	John Paul II, *Tertio Millennio Adveniente*, apostolic letter, Vatican website, November 10, 1994, w2.vatican.va, §33.
"No human sin can erase the mercy of God."	John Paul II, *Veritatis Splendor*, encyclical letter, Vatican website, August 6, 1993, w2.vatican.va, §118.

EIGHTH STATION

"Tears must prevent other tears."	Angelo Comastri, *Way of the Cross at the Colosseum* (Vatican City: Office for the Liturgical Celebrations of the Supreme Pontiff, 2006), accessed July 2, 2019, w2.vatican.va.
"Save the child, not me."	Pontifical Council for the Promotion of the New Evangelization, "A Merciful Mother: St. Gianna Beretta Molla," in *The Saints in Mercy: Pastoral Resources for Living the Jubliee* (Huntington, IN: Our Sunday Visitor, 2015), 69–73.
" … are able to fulfill themselves."	John Paul II, *Canonization of Six New Saints*, homily, Vatican website, May 16, 2004, w2.vatican.va.

NINTH STATION

" … sprinkled the souls that were making their way to God."	"The Message of Fatima" (Vatican City: Congregation for the Doctrine of the Faith, 2000), accessed July 2, 2019, w2.vatican.va.
" … when I was wounded by gun-shots … "	John Paul II, *Crossing the Threshold of Hope*, 221.
" … another hand, Mary's hand, guided the bullet."	André Frossard, *Portrait of John Paul II* (San Francisco: Ignatius Press, 1990), 251.

TENTH STATION

"When he was with the sick and old, he was never in a hurry."	Evert, *Saint John Paul the Great*, 184.
" … the salvific meaning of suffering is revealed before him."	John Paul II, *Salvifici Doloris*, apostolic letter, Vatican website, February 11, 1984, w2.vatican.va, §26.

ELEVENTH STATION

"I have to make it to the end." | Slawomir Oder, *Why He Is a Saint,* 127–128. See also Evert, *Saint John Paul the Great,* 197; and Paterno Esmaquel II, "John Paul to Ratzinger: Should I resign?" *Rappler,* February 26, 2013.

" … the radiant dawn of the Resurrection." | Prayer of Mother Teresa of Calcutta, *L'Osservatore Romano,* August 24, 1992, in Stanisław Dziwisz et al., *Let Me Go to the Father's House: John Paul II's Strength in Weakness* (Boston: Pauline Books and Media, 2006), 36.

"I made a fervent and trusting prayer … " | John Paul II, "Homily of His Holiness John Paul II for the Inauguration of His Pontificate," homily, Vatican website, October 22, 1978, w2.vatican.va.

"Now, I ask him to call me back … " | John Paul II, *L'Osservatore Romano,* April 8, 2005, in Dziwisz, *Let Me Go to the House of the Father,* 36.

TWELFTH STATION

" … people singing prayers outside his window."	Evert, *Saint John Paul the Great*, 200–205; Dziwisz, *A Life with Karol*, 248–260.
" … rather, he 'abandons' himself to the Father … "	John Paul II, *Novo Millennio Ineunte*, apostolic letter, Vatican website, January 6, 2001, w2.vatican.va, §25–26.
" … open up the mystery of liberation through death."	John Paul II, "Remarks by John Paul II After Completing the Stations of the Cross, 1999," Vatican website, April 2, 1999, w2.vatican.va.

THIRTEENTH STATION

" … despite the physical absence."	John Paul II, "Homily at 10th National Eucharistic Congress," Brazil. Cited by Evert, *Saint John Paul the Great*, 140.
" … symbols for baptism and the Eucharist."	Cf. John Chrysostom, "Catechesis 3:13–19," in the Divine Office, Office of Readings for Good Friday.

" … whose heart once beat in unison with hers."	John Paul II, *Ecclesia de Eucharistia*, encyclical letter, Vatican website, April 17, 2003, w2.vatican.va, §56.

FOURTEENTH STATION

" … asking for his intercession."	Dziwisz, *Let Me Go to the Father's House*, 89.
" … he had passed 'from life into life.'"	Dziwisz, *Let Me Go to the Father's House*, 39.
" … and his wish was truly accomplished."	Zuchniewicz, *Miracles of John Paul II*, 178.
" … 'expectation of the resurrection of the body and life everlasting.'"	John Paul II, *Gift and Mystery*, 46–47.
" … an eternal dwelling is made for them in heaven."	"Preface I for the Dead" in "Prefaces from the Roman Missal," Liturgies. net, http://www.liturgies. net/Liturgies/Catholic/ roman_missal/prefaces. htm#dead1. See also 2 Cor 5:1.

Prayer before the Altar

" … the graces we implore, through Christ Our Lord. Amen."

"Prayer for the Intercession of St. John Paul II," Saint John Paul II National Shrine, accessed July 2, 2019, https://www.jp2shrine.org/en/worship/jp2-prayer.html.

More Reading on Saint John Paul II

Pre-Pontifical Works

Wojtyła, Karol. *Collected Plays and Writings on Theater.* Translated by Boleslaw Taborski. Berkeley: University of California Press, 1987.

―――. *Love and Responsibility.* Rev. ed. San Francisco: Ignatius Press, 1993.

―――. *Person and Community: Selected Essays.* 2nd ed. Translated by Theresa Sandok. New York: Peter Lang, 2008.

―――. *Sign of Contradiction.* New York: Seabury Press, 1979.

―――. *The Way to Christ: Spiritual Exercises.* New ed. San Francisco: HarperOne, 1994.

Personal Works

John Paul II. *Crossing the Threshold of Hope.* New York: Alfred A. Knopf, 1994.

―――. *Gift and Mystery: On the Fiftieth Anniversary of My Priestly Ordination.* New York: Doubleday, 1996.

————. *Man and Woman He Created Them: A Theology of the Body.* 2nd printing ed. Translated by Michael Waldstein. Boston: Pauline Books and Media, 2006.

————. *Memory and Identity: Conversations at the Dawn of a Millennium.* London: Orion Books, 2005.

————. *Rise, Let Us Be on Our Way.* New York: Warner Books, 2004.

Pontifical Works

John Paul II. *Pope John Paul II: Documents.* 4 vols. Trivandrum, India: Carmel International Publishing House, 2005.

Other Works on Pope John Paul II

Accattoli, Luigi. *When a Pope Asks Forgiveness: The Mea Culpa's of John Paul II.* Translated by Jordan Aumann. New York: Alba House, 2000.

Benedict XVI. *John Paul II, My Beloved Predecessor.* Boston: Pauline Books and Media, 2007.

Dziwisz, Stanisław. *A Life with Karol: My Forty-Year Friendship with the Man Who Became Pope.* Translated by Adrian Walker. New York: Doubleday, 2007.

Dziwisz, Stanisław, Czesław Drążek, Renato Buzzonetti, and Angelo Comastri. *Let Me Go to the Father's House: John Paul II's Strength in Weakness.* Boston: Pauline Books and Media, 2006.

Evert, Jason. *Saint John Paul the Great: His Five Loves*. Lakewood, CO: Totus Tuus Press, 2014.

Redzioch, Wlodzimierz. *Stories about Saint John Paul II: Told by His Close Friends and Co-Workers*. Translated by Michael J. Miller. San Francisco: Ignatius Press, 2015.

Svidercoschi, Gian Franco. *Stories of Karol: The Unknown Life of John Paul II*. Translated by Peter Heinegg. Liguori, MO: Liguori/Triumph, 2003.

Weigel, George. *Lessons in Hope: My Unexpected Life with St. John Paul II*. New York: Basic Books, 2017.

———. *Witness to Hope: The Biography of Pope John Paul II, 1920–2005*. New York: Harper, 2005.

Zuchniewicz, Pawel. *Miracles of John Paul II*. Translated by Paul Bulas, Fr. Ted Nowak OMI, and Margaret Olszewski. Ontario, Canada: Catholic Youth Studio-KSM, 2006.

About the Author

FATHER HERBERT NIBA CHEO is a priest of the Diocese of Buea, Cameroon. He holds a master's degree in philosophy from the Catholic University of Central Africa, Yaoundé, Cameroon (2010) and a bachelor of divinity degree from the Pontifical Urban University, Rome (2014). He has served as director of the John Paul II Institute of Theology, Buea, Cameroon (2014–2016) and is currently a formator and lecturer in philosophy at St. John Paul II Major Seminary, Bachuo Ntai, Mamfe, Cameroon. He is the author of the book-length interview *Amare et Servire: The Life and Work of Henri Peeters, MHM* (Bamenda, Cameroon: Arise Press, 2014).